DESTINATION MARS

MARS

ROVERS

Ty Chapman

Lerner Publications ◆ Minneapolis

For wonderers and dreamers everywhere

Lerner Publications Company
An imprint of Lerner Publishing Group, Inc.
241 First Avenue North
Minneapolis, MN 55401 USA

For reading levels and more information, look up this title at www.lernerbooks.com.

Main body text set in Aptifer Sans LT Pro.
Typeface provided by Linotype AG.

Designer: Viet Chu **Photo Editor:** Annie Zheng
Lerner team: Martha Kranes

Library of Congress Cataloging-in-Publication Data

Names: Chapman, Ty, author.
Title: Mars rovers / Ty Chapman.
Description: Minneapolis, MN, USA : Lerner Publications, Inc., [2024] | Series:
    Destination Mars. Alternator books | Includes bibliographical references and
    index. | Audience: Ages 8–12 | Audience: Grades 4–6 | Summary: "Space-loving
    readers who wonder what Mars rovers are, what their findings are, and why they
    are important are in for a treat with this book all about the fascinating Mars
    exploration vehicles"— Provided by publisher.
Identifiers: LCCN 2022046124 (print) | LCCN 2022046125
    (ebook) | ISBN 9781728490670 (lib. bdg.) | ISBN 9798765602799 (pbk.) |
    ISBN 9781728496948 (eb pdf)
Subjects: LCSH: Roving vehicles (Astronautics)—Juvenile literature. | Mars—
    Exploration—Juvenile literature.
Classification: LCC TL475 .C48 2024 (print) | LCC TL475 (ebook) | DDC 629.43/543—
    dc23/eng/20221212

LC record available at https://lccn.loc.gov/2022046124
LC ebook record available at https://lccn.loc.gov/2022046125

Manufactured in the United States of America
1-52998-51016-2/13/2023

TABLE OF CONTENTS

INTRODUCTION

ENDLESS CURIOSITY

Rolling through the dust and rock of Mars's surface is the Curiosity rover. Curiosity was launched in 2011. When the rover touched down in Gale Crater, the scientists at the National Aeronautics and Space Administration (NASA) expected it to last about one Martian year, or 687 Earth days. In 2022 Curiosity was still collecting data from the planet's surface.

One of the reasons Curiosity has lasted so long is because of how much scientists have learned about building rovers over many years. From wheels that can roll over rocks twice their size to its efficient power system, many technological improvements have made Curiosity a success. Additionally, hundreds of dedicated engineers work together to keep the rover's many parts functional. They send commands to the rover from 100 million miles (161 million km) away using radio signals.

Curiosity was so successful that Perseverance, launched in 2020, is based on it. Perseverance's upgrades include thicker aluminum wheels, a new operating system, and a longer robotic arm equipped with scientific instruments.

Curiosity and Perseverance have taught us a great deal about Mars. Their discoveries build upon information gathered by their predecessors, Spirit, Opportunity, and Sojourner, as well as rovers from other space programs.

Curiosity's cameras allow it to take selfies.

Retrorockets helped slowly lower Curiosity to Mars's surface so that it could land safely.

CHAPTER 1

WHAT'S A ROVER?

Once the spacecraft comes close enough to its destination, it deploys a lander containing the rover. The lander protects the rover as it plummets through the planet's atmosphere. Because a full-speed crash would destroy the expensive rovers, engineers equip the landers with tools such as parachutes, retrorockets, and airbags to slow them. When the lander has safely reached the planet's surface, the rover emerges from it, and the mission officially begins.

NASA engineers spend months building rovers. They attach airbags and other landing gear.

Scientists cannot launch rovers at any time. Earth and Mars travel at different speeds around the sun, so the distance between the two planets constantly changes. Scientists wait to send spacecraft to Mars until the two planets are close together. This happens about every twenty-six months. A shorter journey means it's less likely for something to go wrong along the way.

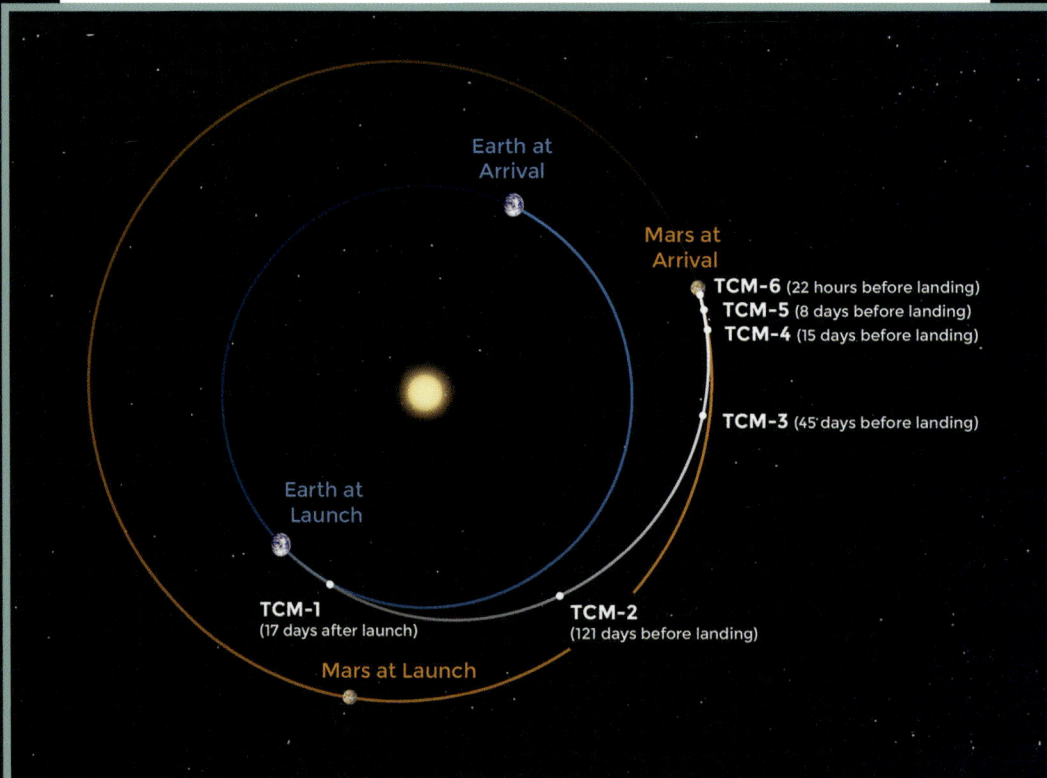

Earth at
Arrival

Mars at
Arrival

TCM-6 (22 hours before landing)
TCM-5 (8 days before landing)
TCM-4 (15 days before landing)

TCM-3 (45 days before landing)

Earth at
Launch

TCM-1
(17 days after launch)

TCM-2
(121 days before landing)

Mars at Launch

This illustration shows the path (*white*) that spacecraft travel from Earth to Mars.

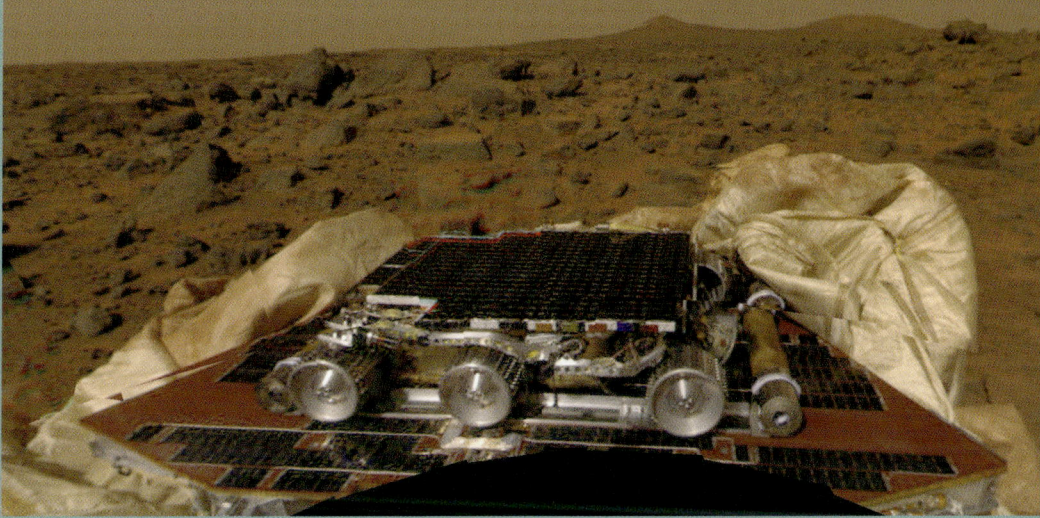

Although Sojourner lasted much longer than scientists predicted, it only traveled about 328 feet (100 m) before it shut down.

ROVING FOR DECADES

NASA's Sojourner landed on Mars in 1997 and was the first successful Mars rover. The rover was about the size of a microwave oven and had very few scientific instruments. While NASA planned for Sojourner to explore for only seven days, the small rover lasted eighty-three days. Like more recent rovers, Sojourner spent most of its time taking pictures of the planet and measuring chemicals. It learned more about what materials are in Mars's soil and atmosphere. The data it collected was the first to ever come from Mars's surface. With Sojourner's success, NASA proved that we could send scientific instruments to another planet and make new discoveries.

CHINA'S ZHURONG ROVER

China's space program landed its first rover on Mars in 2021. The rover, named Zhurong, is equipped with cameras, a radar for scanning beneath Mars's surface, and a weather monitor. It was built to last ninety days but has continued exploring Mars for much longer. Zhurong has been collecting rock and soil samples for a future space mission to take back to Earth. Scientists plan to retrieve Zhurong's samples in 2031.

Zhurong is over 6 feet (1.85 m) tall. Like many rovers, it is powered by solar panels.

Since the 1990s, rovers have continued to grow in size and capability. Spirit and Opportunity, launched in 2003, were both as large as golf carts. The pair were part of the Mars Exploration Rovers mission. Their primary goal was to investigate the planet's rocks and soil for evidence of water. They sported new scientific instruments, such as the rock abrasion tool, which they used to cut into the surface of Martian rocks.

Mars's rocks are reddish because of all the rusting iron on the planet's surface.

Both Spirit and Opportunity far surpassed their expected ninety-day mission lengths. Spirit explored until 2009, when it became trapped in a pit of sand and ran out of power. Opportunity studied the planet until 2015, when a very powerful dust storm blocked its solar panels for too long, and the rover went offline.

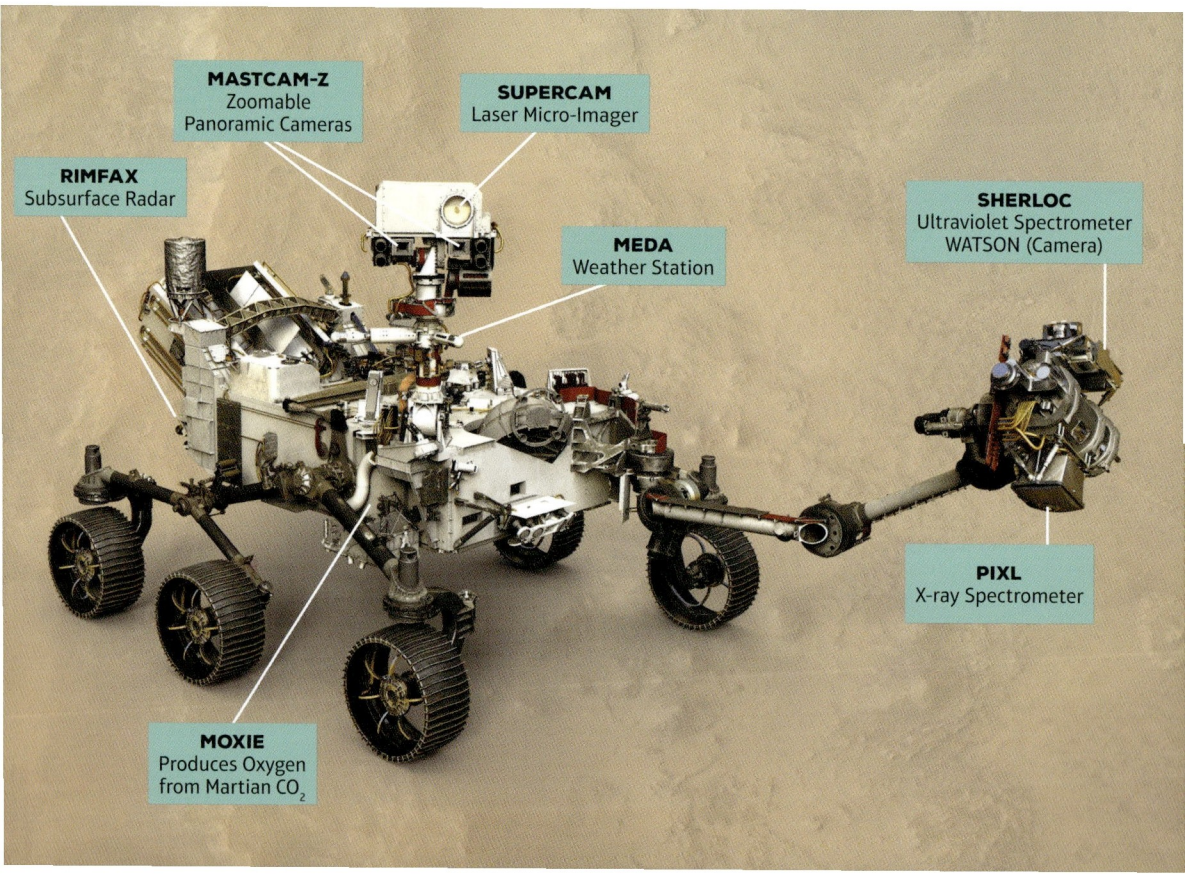

MASTCAM-Z
Zoomable
Panoramic Cameras

SUPERCAM
Laser Micro-Imager

RIMFAX
Subsurface Radar

SHERLOC
Ultraviolet Spectrometer
WATSON (Camera)

MEDA
Weather Station

PIXL
X-ray Spectrometer

MOXIE
Produces Oxygen
from Martian CO_2

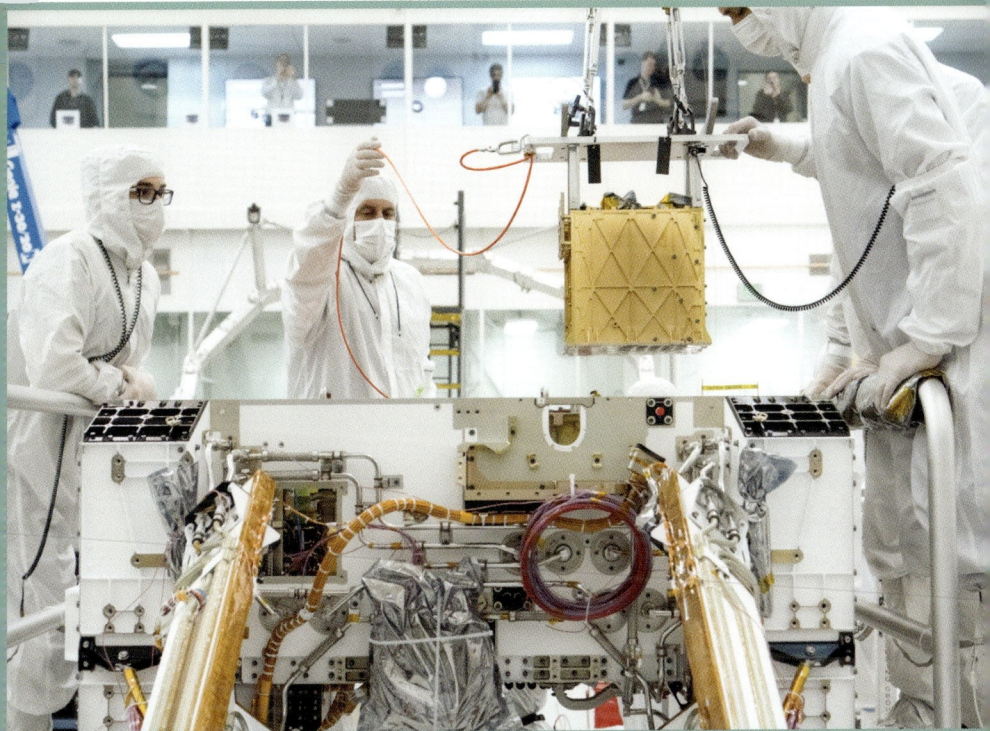
Engineers install MOXIE, the golden box, into Perseverance.

Newer rovers, such as Curiosity and Perseverance, are the size of cars and host an impressive array of instruments. Perseverance's scientific instruments include state-of-the-art cameras and sensors, as well as a coring drill for cutting into rocks. It also carries a new instrument called MOXIE that can convert the toxic gases in Mars's atmosphere into breathable oxygen. If MOXIE is successful, it will be an important tool for any human beings who land on Mars's surface.

In the ancient past, Mars likely had oceans of liquid water.

CHAPTER 2

WHAT HAVE WE LEARNED FROM ROVERS?

Thanks to Rovers using scientific instruments to investigate Mars, we've learned a great deal about the planet. Each of these discoveries will be very important as we seek to land humans on Mars.

As a result of Curiosity's close study of Gale Crater, scientists have discovered there likely was liquid water on Mars's surface in the past. Curiosity also detected materials including sulfur, nitrogen, oxygen, phosphorous, and organic molecules in Mars's rocks and soil. Each of these materials are essential for life. While this discovery is not proof of life, it does mean life on Mars is more possible than scientists previously thought.

Ancient volcanic eruptions on Mars spread chemicals like sulfur across the planet's surface.

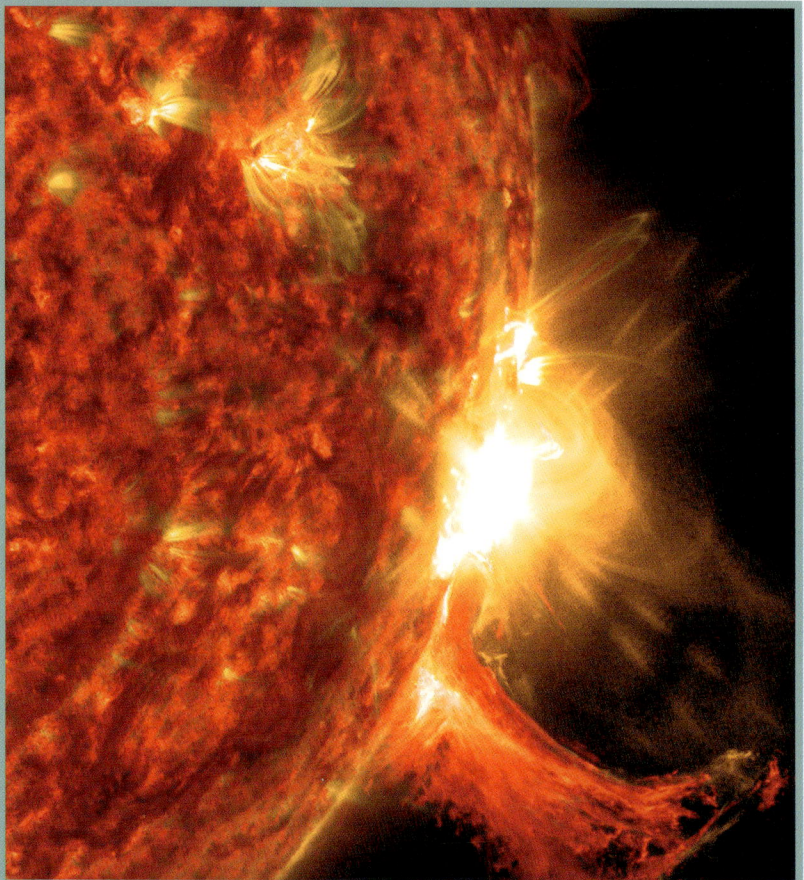

Solar flares create radiation so strong it can damage satellites and other technology orbiting Earth.

SAFETY FIRST

Scientists have learned there are two types of dangerous radiation on Mars. One type is galactic cosmic rays, which are created by exploding stars far away in space. The other type is solar energetic particles, which are created by solar flares. Both types of radiation are made of extremely fast, powerful particles. They are too small to see, but they are very dangerous for humans and other forms of life. Astronauts need special suits and equipment to protect themselves from radiation. These two types of radiation rain down constantly on Mars, making it unsafe for humans to explore without the right protection.

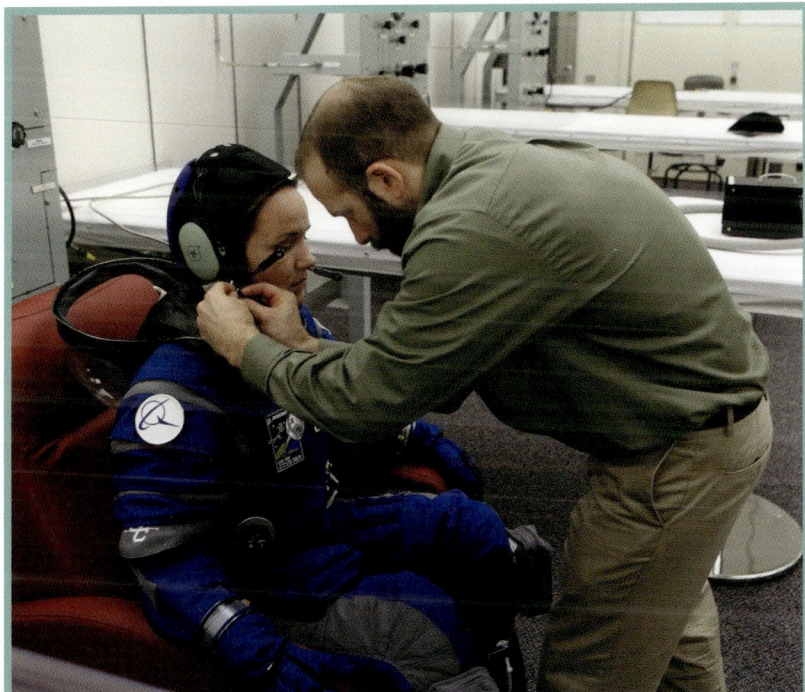

NASA is testing new spacesuits to use for astronauts traveling to Mars.

A NAME FOR EVERY ROVER

Before scientists launch a rover millions of miles away, it needs a name. NASA has a unique tradition for naming these explorers. After Sojourner, named for abolitionist and women's rights activist Sojourner Truth, was launched in 1996, NASA started naming contests open to all US students from kindergarten to twelfth grade. Thousands of kids submit their ideas for a new rover's name, and the winning name becomes official.

Sojourner Truth (1797–1883) spent her life fighting for the rights of women and enslaved people in the United States.

To see a rocket launch up close, you will have to buy tickets from NASA and travel to the Kennedy Space Center in Florida.

HOW TO TEST YOUR ROVER

Perseverance went through extensive testing before being sent to Mars to reduce the chances of anything going wrong during launch, landing, or exploring. Because launching a rocket can be incredibly loud, producing noise of up to 180 decibels, components of the rover could rattle loose or break during takeoff.

Engineers inspect Perseverance before testing it in the sound chamber. The engineers wear special clothes to keep the spacecraft from getting dirty.

To reduce the risk of the rover falling apart, NASA scientists placed Perseverance in a special sound chamber in their laboratory. The chamber was filled with powerful speakers that blasted Perseverance with 143 decibels of sound. While a few small components needed tightening, Perseverance passed the test, proving to scientists that it would survive a trip to Mars.

CRATERS, VOLCANOES, AND RIVERS

Perseverance was deployed to Jezero Crater on a mission to search for evidence of microbial life once existing on Mars. Thanks to Perseverance snapping over 282,000 pictures of a dry riverbed inside the crater, scientists have made unexpected discoveries. The rover captured images of both sedimentary and igneous rocks. Based on the sedimentary rocks, scientists believe that there was once liquid water in the crater. Since igneous rocks form from lava, scientists learned the crater used to be a Martian volcano millions of years ago.

Jezero Crater is 2,300 miles (3,700 km) from Gale Crater. That means Perseverance and Curiosity are about as far apart as the east and west coasts of the United States are from each other.

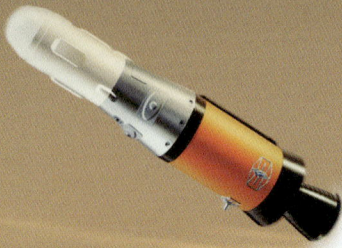

To bring back samples collected by Perseverance, scientists need to figure out how to launch a spacecraft from the surface of Mars. No one has ever done that before.

CHAPTER 3

RACE TO MARS

NASA, the European Space Agency (ESA), and the China National Space Administration (CNSA) all have big plans for the exploration of Mars. NASA's next goal is to work with the ESA to send a spacecraft to Mars to collect the rock and soil samples gathered by Perseverance. The samples would then be brought back to Earth for scientists to study more closely.

The ESA has been preparing to launch a never-before-seen rover for many years. The Rosalind Franklin rover launch, once scheduled for 2020, was delayed because of the COVID-19 pandemic. The rover is equipped with a drill that allows it to dig up to 6.5 feet (2 m) underground, a camera to take pictures beneath and above the surface of Mars, and an onboard laboratory to study samples and search for evidence of Martian life.

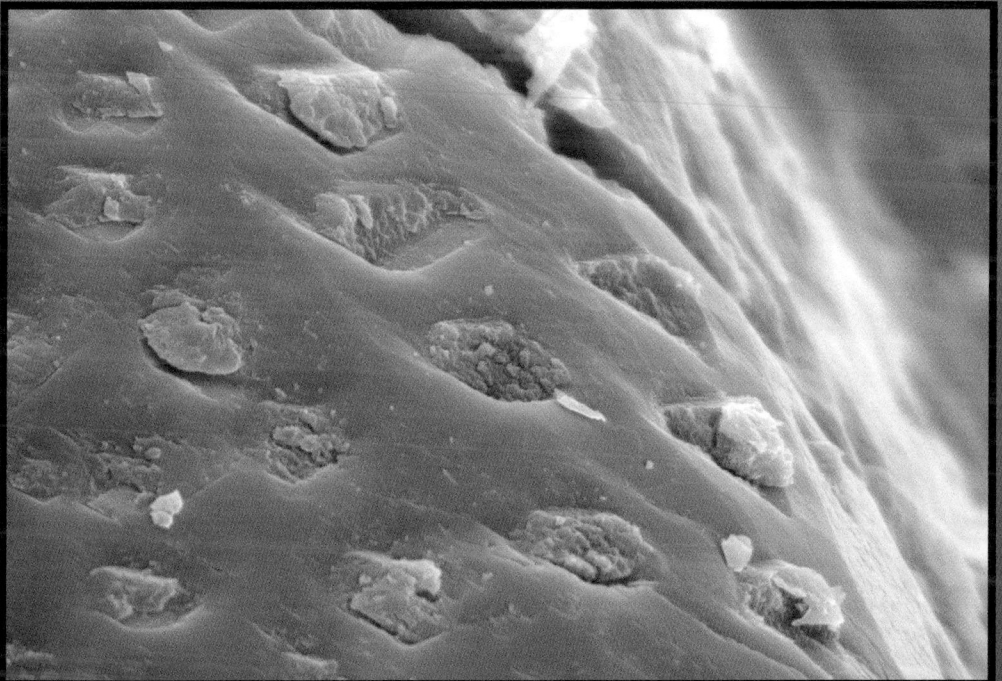

Scientists use microscopes to find fossils created by microbes. They are looking for fossils like these on rocks from Mars.

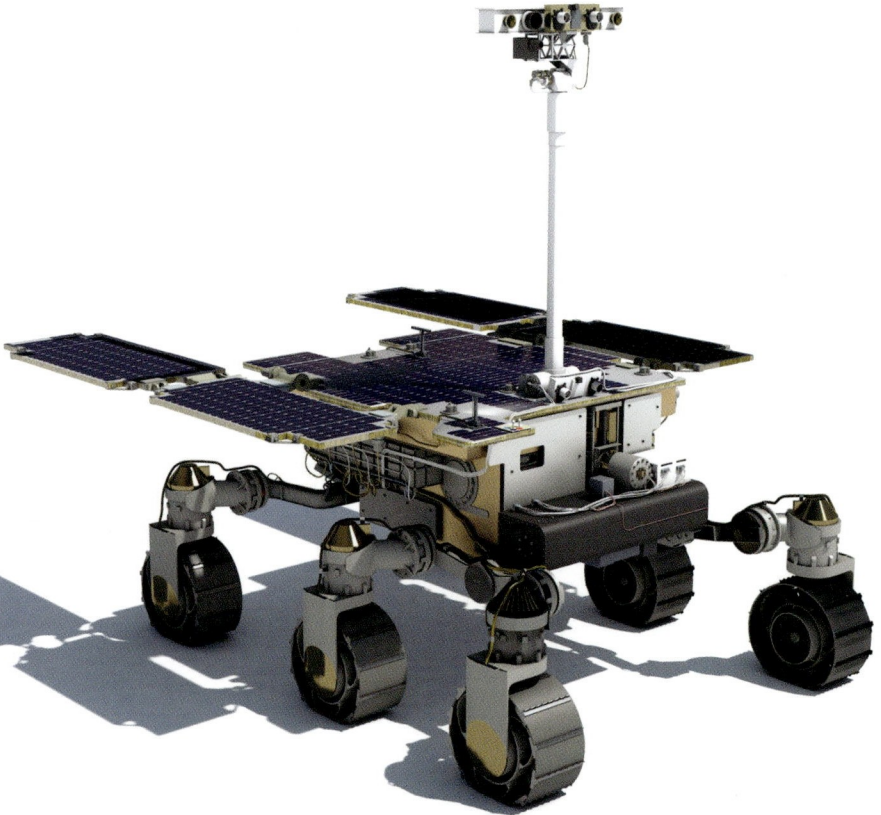

The Rosalind Franklin will search for the chemicals that are the building blocks of life.

Scientists from the ESA and from Russia collaborated on this mission, with Russia providing the rocket and lander. But after Russia invaded Ukraine in early 2022, the ESA decided not to use Russia's rocket. While the rover has passed all its tests for launch, its mission might not begin until 2030.

FROM THE MOON TO MARS

Many space programs and organizations want to be the first to send humans to Mars. While they still need to learn more about Mars's dangers, create protective gear, and test equipment like MOXIE, scientists are already planning missions for astronauts to go to Mars.

On Mars, astronauts can repair broken parts on rovers or help rovers travel across difficult terrain.

Artemis will use the most
powerful rockets ever created
to send humans into space.

When many countries work together, more scientific discoveries are made.

NASA's Artemis mission will build a base camp for astronauts on Earth's moon to conduct more science on the moon's surface than ever before. If Artemis is successful, NASA can use it as a model for similar missions to Mars. CNSA is also joining in the space race to colonize Mars, with ambitious launches of astronaut crews planned for 2033, 2035, 2037, and 2041.

Some private companies working on space technology claim to have plans of landing humans on Mars as soon as 2026 or 2030, but NASA has voiced that this is unlikely. There are still too many unknowns to risk sending humans so soon.

SpaceX is one company that wants to send humans to Mars. It also helps deliver supplies to astronauts on the International Space Station.

Perseverance uses its drills to collect a sample of Martian rock.

Regardless of who manages to land astronaut boots on Martian soil first, the discoveries those astronauts make will benefit all of science. While there are many obstacles standing in the way of human exploration, our rovers hold the key to overcoming them.

Glossary

ambitious: marked by a desire to be successful

colonize: to migrate to and settle in another land or planet

decibel: a unit for measuring the intensity of sound

lander: a space vehicle that is designed to land on the surface of a planet or moon

microbial: relating to microbes (very small living things)

organic molecules: chemical materials that are found in all forms of life on Earth

plummet: to fall quickly

predecessor: something that came before

retrorocket: a small rocket that pushes against the motion of a vehicle, causing it to slow down

solar flare: a burst of energy from the sun

Learn More

Hirsch, Rebecca E. *Mysteries of Mars.* Minneapolis: Lerner Publications, 2021.

Hirsch, Rebecca E. *Space Machines in Action.* Minneapolis: Lerner Publications, 2020.

Kenney, Karen Latchana. *Breakthroughs in Mars Exploration.* Minneapolis: Lerner Publications, 2019.

NASA Mars Exploration: Mars for Kids
https://mars.nasa.gov/participate/funzone/

NASA Space Place: The Mars Rovers
https://spaceplace.nasa.gov/mars-rovers/en/

National Geographic Kids: Mission to Mars
https://kids.nationalgeographic.com/space/article/mission-to-mars

Planets for Kids: Mars Missions—Rovers
https://www.planetsforkids.org/missions/mars-missions-rovers.html

Rusch, Elizabeth. *The Mighty Mars Rovers: The Incredible Adventures of Spirit and Opportunity.* New York: Clarion Books, 2017.

Index

Photo Acknowledgments

Image credits: NASA/JPL-Caltech/ESA/DLR/FU Berlin/MSSS, p. 4; NASA/JPL-Caltech/MSSS, pp. 5, 11; NASA/JPL-Caltech, pp. 6, 8, 12, 13, 20, 22, 29; NASA, pp. 7, 9; Future Publishing/Getty Images, p. 10; Ittiz/Wikimedia Commons (CC BY-SA 3.0), p. 14; Mark Garlick/Science Photo Library/Getty Images, p. 15; NASA Goddard, p. 16; NASA/Cory Huston, p. 17; Library of Congress, p. 18; NASA/Joel Kowsky, p. 19; NASA/Wikimedia Commons PD, p. 21; NASA Image Collection/David McKay/Alamy Stock Photo, p. 23; Adrian Mann/Stocktrek Images/Getty Images, p. 24; Gorodenkoff/Shutterstock, p. 25; NASA/Ben Smegelsky, p. 26; picture alliance/Getty Images, p. 27; NASA/Expedition 39, p. 28. Design elements: ESA/DLR/FU-Berlin (CC BY 4.0).

Front cover: NASA/JPL-Caltech/MSSS.

Back cover: ESA/DLR/FU-Berlin (CC BY 4.0).